Looking Back at
LITTLEBOROUGH

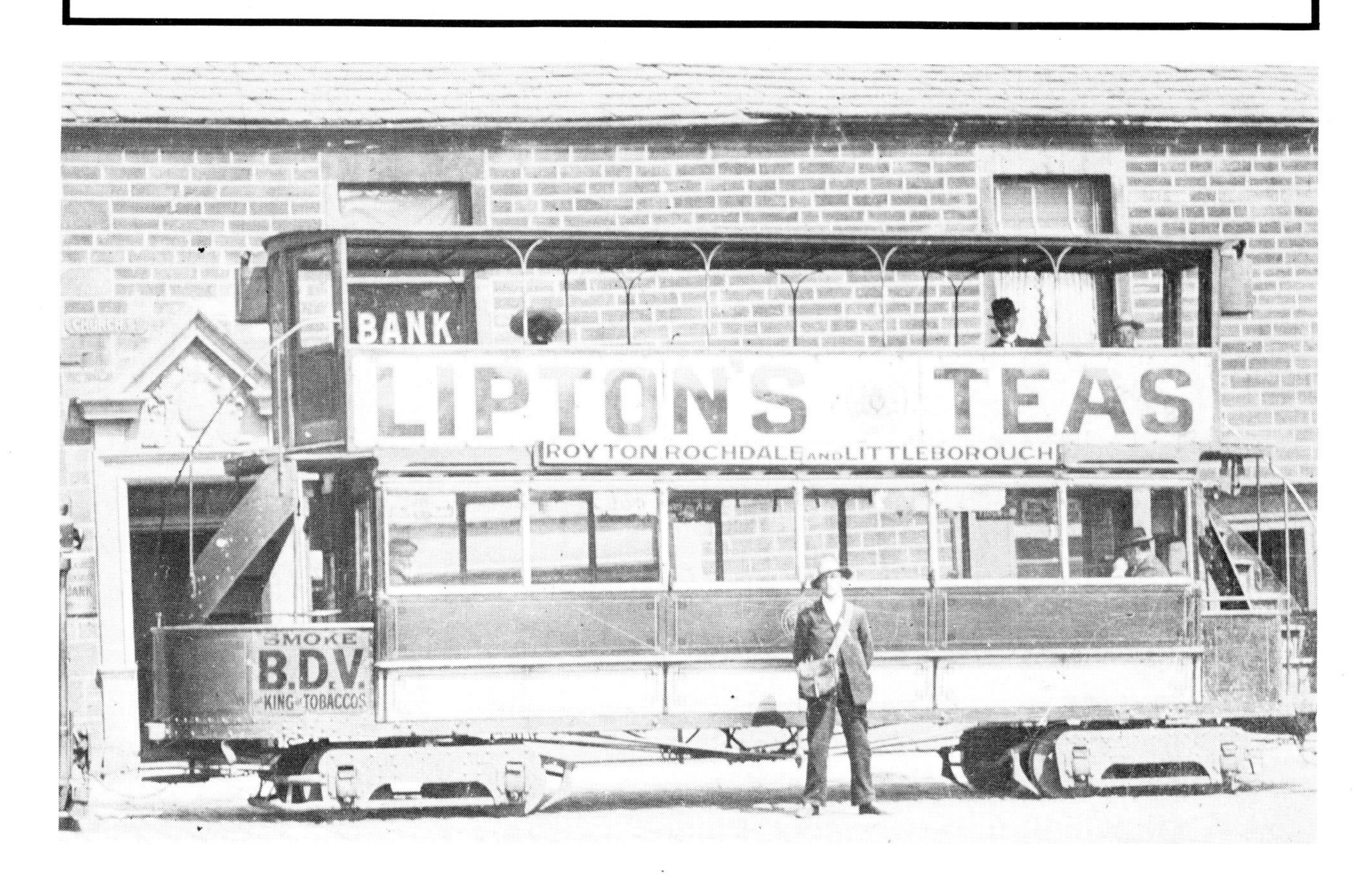

George Kelsall & Keith Parry

Published by George Kelsall
The Bookshop, 22 Church Street
Littleborough, Lancashire

Printed by The Commercial Centre Ltd.,
Hollinwood, Oldham

ISBN 0 9505577 6 5

(Opposite Page) Plan of Littleborough in 1981. Reproduced from the Ordnance Survey and kindly loaned by Rochdale Libraries.

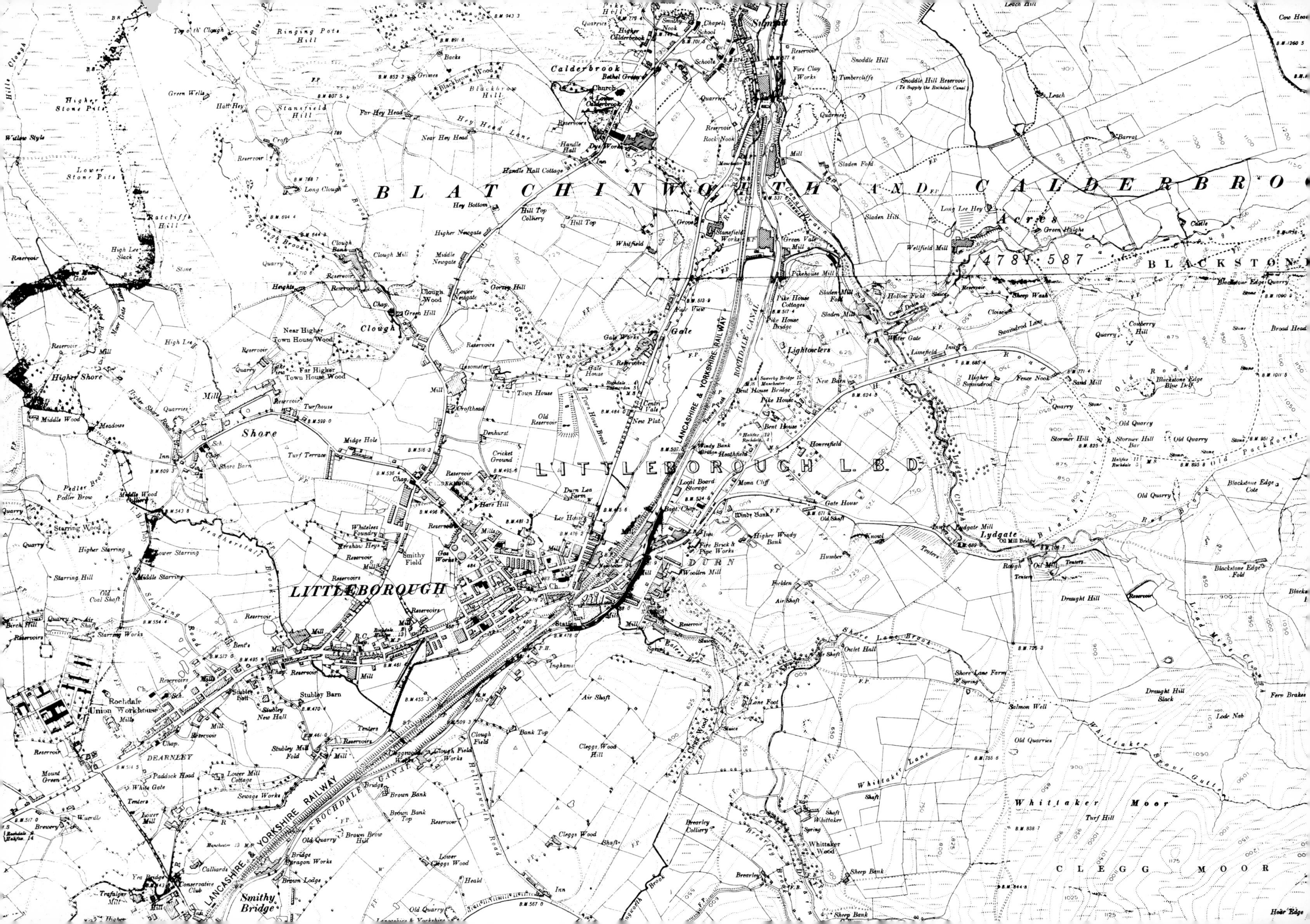
BLATCHINWORTH AND CALDERBRO
LITTLEBOROUGH L. B. D.
LITTLEBOROUGH
BLACKSTON
Calderbrook
Summit
Shore
Clough
Gale
Durn
Lydgate
Lightowlers
Dearnley
Rochdale Union Workhouse
Smithy Bridge
Whittaker Moor
Clegg Moor
Acres
Station
Rochdale Canal
Lancashire & Yorkshire Railway
Higher Shore
Stansfield Hill
Ringing Pots Hill
Blackbrow Hill
Hill Top Colliery
Snoddle Hill
Snoddle Hill Reservoir
Sladen Fold
Sladen Hill
Long Lee Hey
Wellfield Mill
Stormer Hill
Old Quarry
Blackstone Edge Cote
Draught Hill
Turf Hill
Cleggs Wood Hill
Brearley
Sheep Bank
Whittaker Wood
Shore Lane Farm
Salmon Well
Fern Brakes
Lode Nab
Old Quarries
Inghams
Air Shaft
Starring Hill
Higher Starring
Lower Starring
Middle Starring
Pedler Brow
Middle Wood
Stubley Hall
Stubley New Hall
Stubley Barn
Brown Bank
Cleggs Wood
Mount Green
Paddock Head
White Gate
Lower Mill
Trafalgar Mill
Conservative Club
Brearley Colliery
Lane Foot
Oxclet Hall
Smithy Field
Cricket Ground
Town House
Old Reservoir
Denhurst
Crofthead
Mona Cliff
Windy Bank
Higher Windy Bank
Gate House
Hollow Field
Sladen Mill
Cowberry Hill
Broad Head
Fence Nook
Sand Mill
Higher Swaindrod
Swaindrod Lane
Bent House
Pike House
Horrsefield
Near Higher Town House Wood
Far Higher Town House Wood
High Lee
Gorsey Hill
Handle Hall
Far Hey Head
Near Hey Head
Hey Head Lane
Green Wells
Higher Stone Pits
Lower Stone Pits
Long Clough
Ratcliffe Hill
High Lee Slack
Hey Bottom
Higher Newgate
Middle Newgate
Lower Newgate
Clough Wood
Clough Mill
Whitfield
Stansfield Works
Green Vale Mill
Pikehouse Mill
Sheep Wash
Water Gate
Lumefield
Blackstone Edge Fold
Leach
Barrat
Cow Head
Leach Hill
Blackstone Edge Quarry
Knowl
Tenters
Fielden
Whittaker Lane
Brown Bank Top
Brown Brow Hill
Lower Cleggs Wood
Bank Top
Clough Field
Calhards
Paragon Works
Brown Lodge
Smithy Nook
Turf Terrace
Midge Hole
Turfhouse
Meadows
Shore Barn
Rough
Oil Mill
Woollen Mill
Fire Brick & Pipe Works
Hare Hill
Lee House
Durn Lea Farm
Heathfield
Local Board Storage
Gasometer
Gas Works
Whitelees Foundry
Kershaw Heys
Starring Wood
Birch Hill
Starring Works
Old Coal Shaft
Starring Road
Lower Mill Cottage
Sewage Works
Stubley Mill Fold
Yea Bridge
Brewery
Hollingworth Road
Blackstone Edge Old Road
Whittaker Spout Gutter
Hoar Edge
4781 · 587

Introduction

Littleborough began as a scattering of isolated weaving hamlets within the Parish of Hundersfeld, a large area stretching from Rochdale to Todmorden. The Industrial Revolution brought roads, canal and railway, mills, foundries and coal-workings. A town developed, first taking the old names of Blatchinworth and Calderbrook (the areas to the East and West of the River Roch) and only comparatively recently did it take the name of Littleborough.

The combined identity was a formality and for many years the separate communities retained their tightly-knit relationships; people were 'Gatehouse' or 'Shore' and 'Littleborough' meant only the low-lying area around the centre of the town. "Top o'Littleborough" meant not the highest point on Blackstonedge but the junction of Church Street and Hare Hill Road – the highest point for the inhabitants of 'Littleborough'. "Through the Arches" meant the part of the town on the Blackstonedge side of the railway and this term was in common use until very recently.

At the same time, Victorian and Edwardian Littleborough was an expanding town, absorbing hundreds of incoming families and blurring the edges of the old divisions. Three new churches were built – but many more chapels and the Non-Conformist philosophy predominated. The residents of this time knew the photographers well; men who recorded processions, mill-fires, the streets and the very "feel" of the town. Looking at these photographs today we can see that so much has gone – mills, the Whit Walks, the trams and the cobbles. But the smoke pall that enveloped Littleborough for a hundred years has gone too, cleaned stonework glitters in the clear air, trees flourish and flowers grow where they would not grow before.

Old loyalties and allegencies have gone to be replaced by new. More new people have arrived and now Littleborough is bigger – and probably younger – than ever before. And yet 'Littleborough' no longer exists – absorbed now into the Metropolitan Borough of Rochdale in a new administrative county of Greater Manchester.

But 'identity' there is, a growing sense of 'belonging' to something which stretches back through the years of these photographs. And further back – to the sturdily-independent handloom weaver who felt the very hills to be his own.

Keith Parry

Opposite page:

All eyes on the camera in this photograph of the "Top o'Littleborough", the junction between Church Street and Hare Hill Road, taken in about 1903.

Fry's Chocolate
HUDSON'S SOAP
HUDSON'S SOAP
COLMAN'S MUSTARD
COLMAN'S MUSTARD
COLMAN'S STARCH
USE FRY'S PURE COCOA
ROBERT HALL.
GROCER & CORN DEALER
VAN HOUTEN'S COCOA
MAZAWATTEE TEA
MAZAWATTEE TEA
MAZAWATTEE CHOCOLATE
MAZAWATTEE COCOA
BOVRIL
BOVRIL
ROWNTREE'S COCOA
ROWNTREE'S COCOA
ROWNTREE'S COCOA
SPRATT'S PATENT DOG CAKES
SPRATT'S PATENT CHICKEN MEAL
MELOX
MELOX

Littleborough grew rapidly in the second half of the nineteenth century and purpose built shops (as opposed to the converted cottages of Church Street) were erected in Hare Hill Road to serve the needs of the expanding population. Ignoring the quagmire just below the surface, prestige properties were built around the junction with Victoria Street. Within a few years the buildings took on a decided 'tilt' and stayed that way until very recently. The property on the right was rebuilt just before the 1939–45 War, that on the left a little after it. The building on the extreme left remains much as it was when this photograph was taken just before the Great War. The premises on the corner were the Victoria Inn (in fact a Residential Hotel) where, owing to the slope on the floors it was said it was cheaper to get drunk than anywhere else in Littleborough!

This photograph is interesting in that it shows the variety of vehicles on the streets of the town at the time. A handcart from the railway station is followed by a horse-drawn cab which in turn is followed by a motor-car. At the side of the road is a once-familiar flat delivery cart and in the right foreground is a covered hand-cart from which a man appears to be selling newspapers. The squat chimney of the Gas Works is prominent on the left hand side of the road and the old Hare Hill Mill is just visible through the smoke-haze.

ANOS
TEA
TLEBORO'

Until the turn-of-the-century, the entrance to Hare Hill Road was very narrow – little more than an alleyway, between Robert Hall's shop and the two substantial houses illustrated here (Left).

Seed Hill Buildings was built in 1902 but the entrance was still restricted by the old shop on the other corner. The photograph (Below Left) was taken on the occasion of the Coronation of George Vth in 1911.

By the mid 1930s (Below) the old shop had gone and the street had begun to take on some of its present-day appearance. Note too that by this time the old Hare Hill Mill (which restricted the road) had also been demolished.

Only the arched engine house, the 'office' block flanking the gateway and the truncated chimney remain as reminders of the Hare Hill Mill designated 'Littleborough Flannel Factory' here.

The four-storey block constricted Hare Hill Road considerably (see early illustrations of Hare Hill Road) and was demolished in the early 1930s. What we now see is an extension built in CWS days on the open land to the right of the office building.

The old mill had been built by the Newall family and they also, in the 1840s built the Gas Plant across the road. This became the Littleborough Gas Works. The works ceased operations in the 1960s but the gasholders on the site remained until the mid 70s. Now the whole site has been cleared.

Many parts of Littleborough, Calderbrook Road at Caldermoor (Right) and Salley Street (Top Right) look much the same today as they did when these photographs were taken sixty or more years ago.

Rock Nook (left) still had a bare, scarred appearance when this photograph was taken; note the total absence of trees in this once heavily-wooded valley. Calderbrook Terrace, on the left was nicknamed "Red Rag Row" after the number of Liberal voters resident there; although it was not essential to be a Liberal to be a success at "Harvey's" it could be an advantage! The (then) new Summit Board School is just to the right of the terrace and rising above it is the chimney of Sladen Wood – "King's Shed", the first of the Fothergill and Harvey mills. The slimmer chimney to the right is that of the pipe-works which stood alongside the canal at Punchbowl Lock. Material from the demolished works was used to form building blocks; from them the houses at Timbercliffe (which now stand on the hillside behind) were built. The canal steps down in front of Rock Nook Mill and a railway signal box is just visible in the centre right of the picture.

Gordon Harvey (Left) has been described as "Enlightened Millowner, Benefactor and Disappointed Man"; he described himself as "A Radical who is prepared to act on Liberal lines". His connection with Littleborough began in 1879 when, at the age of 21 he arrived to take charge of Fothergill and Harvey's weaving shed at Sladen Wood. He lived first at Sladen Wood House (where Jessie Fothergill, the daughter of his Father's late partner had lived) but in 1903 he and his brother Ernst, who had recently married, moved to Townhouse (Below) which had been the home of the Newall family.

His political career began when he was elected to the newly-formed Lancashire County Council in 1889 and his interest in education led him to start the long battle to establish 'National' schools in Littleborough. After a disappointment in 1900 when he was labelled 'pro-Boer' he was elected to Parliament as Member for Rochdale at the Liberal landslide election of 1906.

Harvey was an enlightened millowner, at least half a century ahead of his time. He instituted canteens for his workpeople, proposed a measure of smoke control in 1910, instituted pension, welfare and educational facilities for his workpeople and built houses for them. He was also a pioneer environmentalist. He landscaped the areas around the Fothergill and Harvey Mills and, in 1919 was responsible for the formation of the quaintly-named "Beautiful Littleborough Society". It is due to this society's efforts that Littleborough has its 'green heart', unusual in Lancashire milltowns.

He was a committed European and firmly opposed to conflict and it is said that the Great War broke both his health and his spirit. But it was he, in a speech at Bacup in 1916 who first used the term "League of Nations". His failing health led to his retirement from Parliament before the election at the end of the War and on November 22nd, barely a week after the Armistice he wrote a farewell letter to his constituents in which he said:– ". . . and now a task infinitely more delicate remains to be accomplished; I mean that great change of mind and heart and soul all over Christendom which shall end war and league the nations in a common purpose".

" . . . of woods and groves and rushing rills,
Delightful mansions and gardens gay
Enrobed in all the pride of smiling May."

So wrote a local poet of the Littleborough he saw in the early years of the 19th century. Mansions there were, the modest but sturdy homes of the 'native' families of the area, the Stotts of Benthouse (Left), the Beswick-Royds' of Pike House (Below Left) and the Rhodes' and Lightowlers of Windybank (Below Right).

But it was the millowning families of the later years of the century who were to build Littleborough's imposing residences. Now, not a single member of these families still lives in Littleborough and in many cases their homes have gone too.

(Opposite Page)

The Cleggs lived at Shore House (Top Left), close by the mill they owned, and the mill was unusual in that it carried out all processes, spinning as well as weaving and, in later years marketed its product under the name "Shore Sheets". James Taylor Rogers who had interests in the Hall and Rogers Pipe Works at Smithy Bridge lived at Calder Cottage (Top Right), Hare Hill Road, a house later owned by 'Miss Daisy' a sister of the three MacGills – all long-serving doctors in the area.

Wellington Lodge (Bottom Left) and Hare Hill House were both the property of the Newall family at one time of Townhouse. Hare Hill House became the Offices of the Littleborough UDC in 1900 and Wellington Lodge, derelict for many years was demolished. Some of the material from it was used in the construction of the houses which now stand on the site. Jessie Fothergill, author of several novels depicting life in the (allegedly) ficticious villages of the industrial North lived at Sladen Wood House (Bottom Right); this was also the first Littleborough home of Gordon Harvey. This house, too, has been demolished.

HOUSE

WELLINGTON LODGE

Motor Cars were a rarity in Edwardian Littleborough. The first car in the area (Left) was owned by Edward Taylor of the firm of E. Taylor and Company of Ebor Street. Taylor's were well-known local builders who were responsible for much of the property in the Newall Street and Central Avenue areas. They also built the extensions that made up the Victoria Station in Manchester we see today. They had also built, thirty years earlier, an experimental terrace of houses (Taylor Terrace) in concrete block.

The splendid open tourer (Below) was suitably photographed complete with smartly dressed chauffeur outside Townhouse in about 1910. It has been suggested that this Wolseley was owned by A. J. (later Sir Alfred) Law of Honresfeld, but the location suggests it may have been the property of Ernst or Gordon Harvey.

(Opposite Page) Posing proudly and in the fashion of the time, Messrs. Watkins Speke and Jas Alletson Snr. are here seen with "Victoria".

Steam-powered road engines bridged the gap between the heavy work horse and the modern lorry. This engine – genuinely a "steam roller" was the property of the Urban District Council Highways Department and was affectionately nicknamed "Big Ike". Road-making and maintenance were a simple but laborious process; tar was melted and poured on the surface, chippings were scattered and then Big Ike came along ponderously rolling back and forth until the final effect was satisfactory.

Big Ike is seen here outside the White House at the top of Blackstonedge and turning a great beast like this round was not a matter of a straightforward three-point turn. The driver and fireman needed plenty of space and time and had probably turned the engine in the inn yard closely watched, it seems, by the landlord of the time, James Palmer.

VICTORIA

The battle to establish 'National' schools in Littleborough was long and bitterly fought. The Education Act of 1870 permitted local authorities to set up 'National' or 'Board' Schools – an area previously controlled by the churches or private bodies. Attempts to bring in the new form of education met with implacable opposition from the Established Church, led by the formidable Rev. Doctor Salts, Vicar of Littleborough.

The main advocate of National Education was Gordon Harvey but the vote at each of the Public Meetings was lost until he rallied the support of the Non-Conformists in the town; Littleborough's Central Board School has the dubious reputation of being the very last school in the country to have been sanctioned under the 1870 Act.

Opened in 1901, it is of remarkably advanced design, as were the satelite schools at Smithy Bridge and Summit. The illustration of the Summit Board School (Left) is particularly interesting. Stansfield estate now spreads over the hillside behind, obscuring the view of the spire of St. James' Church.

(Below) Littleborough Central Board School seen from the Council Offices

Durn was a heavily industrialised area when this photograph was taken about 1910. Uber Mill stands between the canal and Halifax Road and on the other side of the road is Frankfort Mill. Across the canal the chimney of Durn Foundry rises above the (then) new Branch Co-op at Durn, built in 1906. The building beyond the foundry (with the curious clerestory roof) was, at one time, the local mortuary and stood on the site of Coggeswell's Boatyard. Just out of sight to the right of the picture were Durn Pipeworks, the Durn Mill of A. J. Law, Heap's West View Mill and the mill and colliery workings in the Ealees valley.

The whitewashed arches of the canal bridges stand out against the smoke haze; merging with the haze are the chimneys of the mills further up the valley. From the left we see the twin chimneys of Gale Print Works and a little further away that of Grove Mill. The chimney of Kershaw's Mill in Lydgate Clough is just visible above the shoulder of the hill.

Uber Mill was the scene of a disastrous fire in 1916 (Below) when part of it collapsed on to Frankfort Cottage alongside. Frankfort Mill itself closed in the Depression years in the 1930s and never reopened. Heap's West View Mill also closed, was used to house service personnel during the 1939–45 War and was later demolished to make way for housing. Foundry, Pipeworks and Colliery are long gone and the Saxon House housing development stands on the site of the Filter Beds between West View and the canal.

The way the sunlight is falling suggests that this photograph was taken in the early afternoon and judging by the lines of washing it must have been Monday!

Methodism began in Littleborough with the visits of John Wesley and William Grimshaw to Deanhead (now Summit) in 1747 and 1749. Meetings were first held in the homes of the adherents and only later, when funds allowed, were specially constructed buildings used. Methodism began inside the Church of England (Grimshaw had been, in fact, Curate at Todmorden and was then the Rector of St. Michael's, Haworth) and the principle was that the congregation attended the local church first then moved on to extra teaching and preaching to the home of one of the members or to a specially-constructed 'preaching house'.

But churches were few and far between; to get to the Littleborough church from Deanhead for instance, the worshipper of the mid 1700s would have had to pick his way through the marshy fields alongside the river or go up to the Calderbrook road and round by way of Gorsey Hill, down to Townhouse and then through the fields to the village.

At the same time the population was expanding, but it was the handloom weaving villages like Calderbrook, Shore and Rakewood that were growing – locations well away from the old church in the valley bottom. Strangely, though, the first non-conformist place of worship to be built was in the village of Littleborough, just across the river from the old church (established in 1471 and, by then in a state of disrepair); the Dissenters Chapel, known by the splendid name of "The Methodical Piazza" (Left) was erected in 1806–9.

Possibly spurred on by the sight of the splendid new chapel across the river the Church Authorities rebuilt Holy Trinity on a site a few yards away to the North and the first portion of the present building, the Nave, was erected in 1820. The chancel was added in 1888.

The construction of the railway viaduct virtually overhead caused problems in the Methodical Piazza, it was little used after 1850 and closed by the mid 1860s. Coincidentally, it was not until this time that the second Church of England building to serve the growing area (St. James the Great, Calderbrook) was opened by which time there were well over a dozen Non-Conformist places of worship in the district and one was already closing!

The Congregationalists had held their first meetings in a cottage on the Todmorden road at Summit and, in 1834 built the (again) splendidly-titled "Ebenezer Independent

Congregational" (Above). At the time this was convenient for the congregation but in the 1870s 'Littleborough' Congregationalists, faced with the long walk up to Summit decided to build their own church (now the United Reformed) in Victoria Street.

The Deanhead Methodists, even though their meetings had begun in the middle years of the 18th century were not in a position to build their own chapel (Temple) until 1839; in the next forty years such chapels proliferated until every small community in the area had one – sometimes more – to cater for the needs of the local adherents. Summits (always a 'separate' community) had three – Temple, the grandly-named Mount Gilead on Calderbrook Road and at the bottom of Temple Lane the surviving Primitive Methodists. Clough, Shore, Smithy Bridge, Dearnley, Featherstall, Stubley, even remote Rakewood had their chapels and each acted as a community centre, a focus for local debate and a teaching establishment as well as a place of worship.

In the centre of what had now become a town, two enormous (and almost identical) chapels and Schools were built, the "Free Church" in Church Street and the Wesleyan Methodists in Victoria Street. Both were prominent in the life of the community and the 'Free Church Schools' were important in the days before National Education was established.

The smaller chapels – Zion at Caldermoor and Mount Gilead for instance were kept going by the efforts of a small number of people – often simply a single family – and by the late 1920s it was generally accepted that some of them would have to close and a conference in 1932 formalised the move. Gradually the chapels were closed, some converted to other uses, others demolished. The Free Church was an early victim, closed in the 1930s, used as a "British Restaurant" during the 1939–45 War then converted to industrial use.

Zion, Caldermoor, was another early conversion as was Featherstall but at least they survived; Mount Gilead, Rakewood, Shore, Smithy Bridge and Victoria Street have been demolished.

The Baptists, who had been allied with Ogden, Newhey rather than Rochdale and had met in a cottage at Durn, built their first corrugated iron "Particular Baptist" chapel on Blackstonedge Road in 1880. A few years later they replaced it with a new building in a fine style. This, too, has been converted to industrial use. Only the comparatively new Dearnley Methodists on New Road, Greenhill at Clough Road and Summit Primitive Methodists survive intact and the Littleborough Congregational Church continues as the United Reformed. The Ebenezer Congregational and Stubley Methodist buildings survive but are no longer in use.

Ironically, the original Dissenters' Chapel survived longer than many and it was not until the 1950s that an act of vandalism by Officialdom resulted in its demolition. Had this not been allowed the Methodical Piazza (a dozen years older than the present Parish Church) would have been the oldest place of worship in Littleborough.

PLAN OF THE VISITORS

OF THE

WESLEYAN SUNDAY SCHOOL UNION,

FOR THE ROCHDALE CIRCUIT,

1859.

PLACES.	Hour.		MAY.				June	July	AUGUST.				OCT.	
	M.	A.	8	15	22	29	19	17	7	14	21	28	16	3
ROCHDALE		1½			20 19							16 18		
CHURCH-STILE		1½		10 11						29 17				
BAMFORD	9½				12 14						8 7			
BROADLANE	9½				4 6							14 5		
LOWERPLACE		1½				5 8					9 19			
CASTLETON-MOOR	9½						2 3				1 22			
WARDLE	9			1 7								20 4		
MILNROW	9½			9 22						11 12				
LITTLEBOROUGH				13 15							21 23			
TEMPLE	9½					16 28					13 17			
HEALEY-STONES	9½					17 18						24 25		
LANEHEAD	9½				21 24							28 27		
GRAVEL-HOLE	9			29 27				26 5					4 7	
RAKEWOOD	9½				25 23			3 6				26 29		11 16

VISITORS' NAMES,
AND RESIDENCES.

1. C. Barker, Roach-place
2. R. H. Cubitt, Moss
3. J. Constantine, Yorkshire-street
4. J. Longbottom, Rochdale
5. Joseph Handley, Rochdale
6. Hy. Booth, do.
7. Rh. Baxter, do.
8. T. Patchett, do.
9. James Turner, do.
10. J. Milward, Bamford
11. J. Lord, Broadlane
12. E. Lord, Lowerplace
13. J. Butterworth, do.
14. S. Stansfield, Castleton-moor
15. J. Halstead, do.
16. James Hartley, Wardle
17. F. Howarth, do.
18. H. Lord, Littleborough
19. J. Mills, do.
20. R. Maskew, Temple
21. Eli Crossley, do.
22. James Brierley, Healey-stones
23. James Shepherd, do.
24. J. Buckley, Gravel-hole
25. Thomas Lord, do.
26. C. Harrison, Milnrow
27. B. Sutcliffe, do.
28. J. Sutcliffe, Rakewood
29. J. Handley, Lanehead

Every Visitor is expected to fulfil his own appointment, or if prevented, to provide a substitute from the Plan.

The Visitors are requested to attend the Half-Yearly Meeting of the Committee, to be held in Rochdale, on Friday, October 21st, 1859, at Seven o'clock in the Evening.

It is the duty of the Visitors to open the Schools with Singing and Prayer—inspect the system of teaching—give a suitable address to Teachers and Scholars—and whenever practicable, assemble the Teachers at the close of the School, for friendly conversation on the subject of Teaching, &c., &c.

The Superintendants are particularly requested to give special attention to the Visitation of their respective Schools, by duly announcing the appointment on the preceding Sabbath, urging the full attendance of Teachers, and making any further arrangements to render the occasion interesting.

R. H. CUBITT,
JOSEPH CONSTANTINE, } SECRETARIES.

E. WRIGLEY AND SON, PRINTERS BY "STEAM POWER," ROCHDALE.

(Top Left) Zion Chapel, Caldermoor.
(Top Right) Temple Methodist.
(Bottom Left) Mount Gilead, Calderbrook.
(Bottom Right) Victoria Street Wesleyan Methodist.

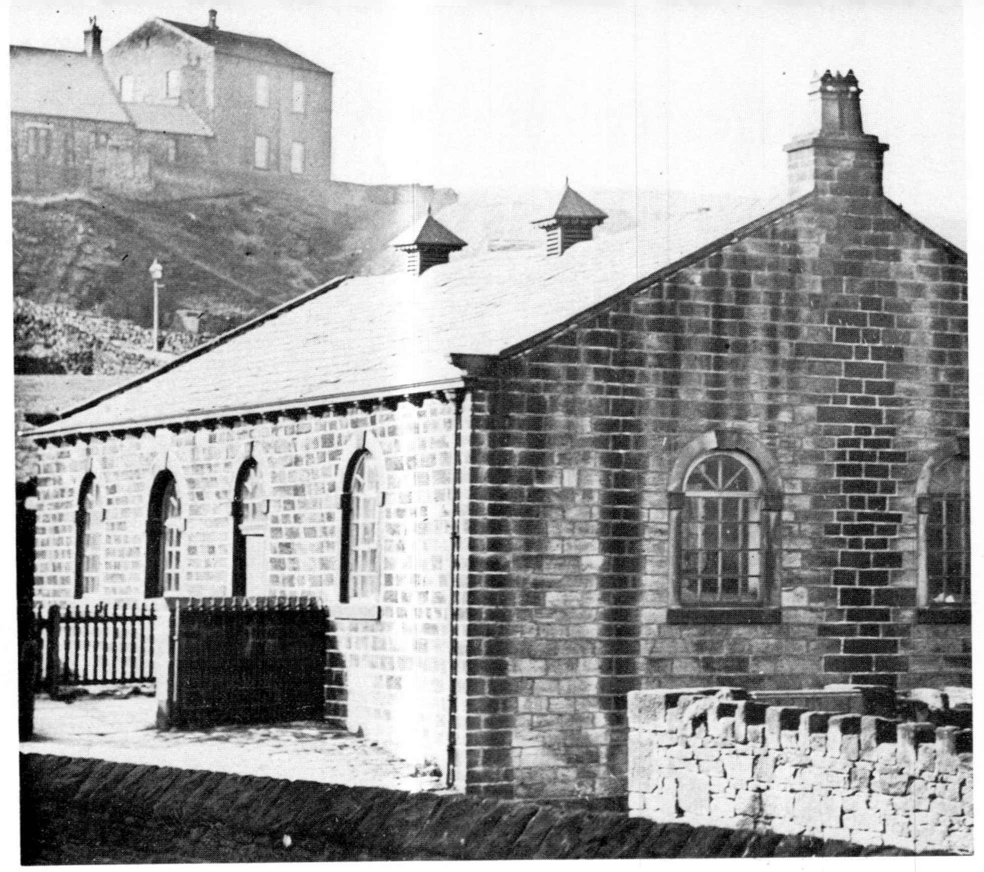

(Left) Durn Particular Baptist.
(Right) Dearnley Methodist.
(Bottom Left) Church Street United Methodist.
(Bottom Right) "The Methodical Piazza".

The spinning of wool was mechanised, using water power, long before weaving and in the early years of the 19th century villages like Calderbrook flourished as centres for the handloom-weaving industry. These cottages at Smithy Nook on what was then the main road to Todmorden (Right) were typical of their type, as Calderbrook was typical of such communities throughout the South Pennines. Each cottage had its weaving room on the upper floor with the characteristic wide window to catch all the available light. Terraces such as these, expanding as the need arose were common but the single unit like Old Mill Cottage (Left) was by no means unusual.

The coming of the steam-powered loom and the purpose-built mill put an end not only to handloom weaving but to a whole way of life – that of the proudly-independent handloom weaver. Gaslight meant that fixed hours could be worked all the year round and the mill itself set the pace and conditions of work. The weaver had set his own pace, working at home surrounded by his family, often dealing with a cloth merchant who supplied the yarn and bought back the finished product; some weavers in fact worked entirely independently, slinging the finished cut across the shoulders and tramping off along the old packhorse road to sell the cloth in the Piece Hall at Halifax.

Weaving by hand lingered on until the 1840s but faced with the fast, efficient and therefore economic power looms the handloom weavers were in dire straits. A recently-discovered entry in the 1851 Census returns for the Hollingworth Workhouse lists one inmate's profession as handloom weaver.

In Samuel Bamford's book "Walks in South Lancashire" the following conversation is recorded between "A Gentleman" and a handloom weaver resident at Smithy Nook, possibly in the cottages illustrated above.

Gentleman: *And how much may you have for weaving a yard of calico?*

Weaver: *A yard, mon? They'n so much a Cut.*

Gentleman: *And how many yards are there in a Cut?*

Weaver: *Why! Theer's thirty yards i'th'Smithy Nook Cal'; and they'n bettin fro' a shillin' to eighteen pence a Cut: that at a shillin'll be Nowt a yard, will it neauw?*

Faced with an unidentified photograph (Left) and little (in this case no) information, the local historian must try to establish the occasion by a process, first, of elimination. It is clearly a Great Occasion, important enough for men to risk life and limb to climb on to the roofs of the buildings overlooking The Square; there are banners – but not the kind of Church and Chapel banners associated with Whit Walks, so it must have been a national, rather than religious occasion. The flags and bunting tend to confirm this. The crowd is packed into The Square and a man is addressing them from a rostrum on the right.

Next, the date. There are no tram-wires, so this must have been before the electric trams were extended into The Square in the summer of 1905. The building on the extreme left hand side of the photograph has a pitched roof; Seed Hill Buildings, which now stand on this site were erected in 1902 and have a flat roof – so it must be before that. The pole in the background carries a number of telephone wires and – importantly, space for more, so we can narrow the date to somewhere between 1890 and 1900.

During that decade, Littleborough was made and Urban District and this could be the actual occasion of Incorporation. At the end of the decade came the Boer War and there were at least two occasions of national rejoicing – the Relief of Ladysmith and the Relief of Mafeking in January and May 1900 respectively. There was, however, the Diamond Jubilee in 1897.

The time of year and time of day can be established. The sun is shining and some people are in white dresses; others are using umbrellas as sun-shades, so it must be summer time (which rules out the Relief of Ladysmith). The angle of the light suggests the sun was high in the sky – as it is in the early afternoon at Midsummer.

Queen Victoria's Diamond Jubilee was celebrated on June 22nd (virtually Midsummer) in 1897 – and legend has it that Her Majesty the Queen Empress always had good weather for her State Occasions!

The Beacon Fire erected on Blackstonedge to celebrate Queen Victoria's Diamond Jubilee and photographs of the beacon during construction. 75 tons of materials were used for the beacon – all of which had to be hauled up Blackstonedge to the White House and then transported along the Broadhead Drain to the site at the top of the Roman Road. A similar if smaller beacon was built for the Silver Jubilee of George Vth in 1935 but the one planned to celebrate the Silver Jubilee in 1977 had to be abandoned due to the recurrance of moor fires still burning underground after the drought summer of the year before.

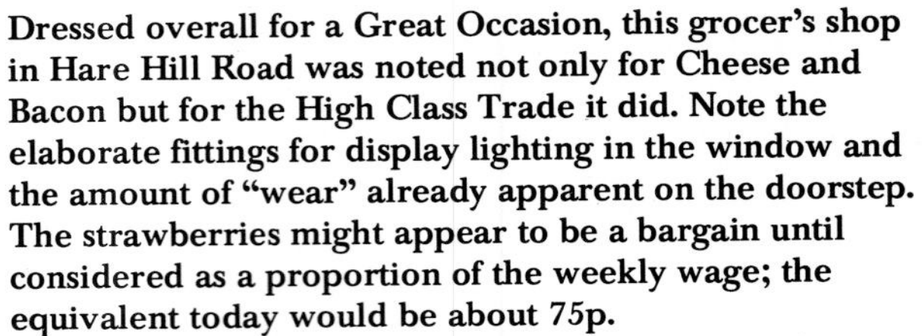

Dressed overall for a Great Occasion, this grocer's shop in Hare Hill Road was noted not only for Cheese and Bacon but for the High Class Trade it did. Note the elaborate fittings for display lighting in the window and the amount of "wear" already apparent on the doorstep. The strawberries might appear to be a bargain until considered as a proportion of the weekly wage; the equivalent today would be about 75p.

Boaters and Bowlers abound in the photograph (Below) taken, one suspects on a Whit Friday. Girls sport white dresses, some boys (unwillingly perhaps) wear frilly lace collars. The band, instruments raised, command attention and the small boys turn towards it. One, shunned perhaps on account of his kilt turns away on the edge of tears (or has posterity caught him in the act of picking his nose?).

The pipes stacked on the hillside identify the location as Summit. A pipeworks stood on a cramped site alongside the canal and just above Punchbowl Lock. The site was taken over by Fothergill and Harvey and waste material from the plant was used to build the houses at Timbercliffe on the hillside above.

In this panoramic view (Right) looking West across the valley from above Timbercliffe the 'new' Temple Methodist Chapel dominates the centre of the picture. Just to the left is the older chapel on the opposite side of Temple Lane. The scattering of old weaving cottages (Paul Row on Temple Lane, those on Calderbrook Road itself and those at Higher Calderbrook) is very apparent, as in the all-important Mawrode Lane linking the three roads to the main road in the valley bottom.

Mount Gilead Chapel is on the right and although St. James' Church is there the Vicarage alongside has not yet been built. The scarring of the landscape brought about by stone-quarrying and the building of the Summit Tunnel (some sixty years before this photograph was taken) is very obvious. The chapels have gone now and much of the land between Temple Lane and Calderbrook Road is taken up by housing.

On the site (where Church Street becomes Featherstall Road) rose Python Mill, surely one of the best proportioned examples of such structures. Initially it was an asbestos factory but was later taken over by the Dutch *Breda Visada Company* who used it to manufacture 'Artificial Silk' – more properly Viscose-Rayon Fibre. The company appointed a Dutch manager who was marooned in Littleborough throughout the 1939–45 War. During the war the one-time maintenance shop for the factory was turned over to manufacturing axles for Churchill Tanks and, presumably on account of the Netherlands Connection received a visit from Prince Bernhard – another exile in Britain at the time.

Ultimately, the ownership was passed to British Enka who closed the factory. Much of it has now been demolished and the Rowlinson Trading Estate now stands on the site, – an interesting example of how the manufacturing environment of Littleborough has changed in the past 70 years.

(Left) In 1907 a photographer recorded this everlastingly-popular event, the spectacular felling of a mill chimney. 'New' mill was in fact, old, but new in the sense that it represented the new generation of mills, powered by steam and built remote from a source of water-power.

(Opposite Page) Girls in wide-brimmed hats and boys in knickerbockers (and most of both in clogs) gaze curiously at the photographer across the road – as they always seem to do in such photographs. A shopkeeper, hands characteristically clasped in front of him leans up against his shop doorway and a woman leans out of an upstairs window. The nearer houses have neat cast-iron railings and the ones further away proclaim their Superior Quality (justifying their nickname "Tall Hat Row") with lavishly-lace-draped bay windows as well as iron railings. A tram, Littleborough-bound from Summit intrudes into the picture and a cheeky girl is captured for ever at the moment of skipping back on to the pavement – perhaps after running across the road to make a 'funny face' into the lens.

A street-scene that could be anywhere any time in the decade before 1914, but this is Todmorden Road, Littleborough.

An Edwardian Album

(Top Left) Cycle Parade 1909.
(Top Right) Calderbrook Church and Vicarage
(Bottom Left) Workers at Blackstonedge Quarry.
(Bottom Right) Littleborough's first taxi.

Above) Steam-powered barge at Long Lees Lock, Summit.
Top Right) Family group at Leach Rock.
Bottom Right) "The Cottage Homes".

(Above) Littleborough Park circa 1902.
(Right) Farm workers at Benthouse.

The newly-formed Urban District of Littleborough's status was confirmed by a Carnegie Free Library in 1901. There was no such thing as self-selection in the early days. An indicator showed the books available, the would-be borrower checked the indicator with a catalogue, approached the Librarian and the Librarian brought the selected book from the shelves.

On the left was the Reading Room with its selection of newspapers and periodicals and on the right was the Royds Library containing books from the Beswicke-Royds home, Pike House. This library was only available to students and those who had paid a fee in excess of the normal library membership fee.

The library had been built as an extension to Hare Hill House and the trophies hanging on the walls were once used to decorate the house itself.

Lacking the traditional Squirearchy or landed gentry, Littleborough could nonetheless rely on the millowners to encourage and support local fund-raising projects. Law, of Durn and Lydgate Mills, Clegg of Shore and the Valentines of Victoria Dyeing Company, Clegg Hall were all 'Church' and could be relied upon to assist church functions, as could the local doctors. All were represented on the various Bazaar committees either personally or by their Ladies.

Significantly, there is no mention of the Harveys in the Bazaar Handbook although Gordon Harvey was already MP for Rochdale and well-known for his philanthropy. This may have been due to the rift that occurred between Harvey and the Vicar, the Rev. Doctor Salts during the long battle to secure 'National' education in Littleborough. Harvey won the battle for the schools by gaining the support of the Non-Conformist vote and although Liberalism and Non-Conformism often went together the Harvey family were Church of England; 'Church Parade' as the family and their servants made their way from Townhouse to Holy Trinity on Sunday morning was a familiar sight.

The purpose of this mammoth three-day "Grand Floral Bazaar" was to raise £1500 to build an extension to the Parish Church School.

(Above) A group of Littleborough's most influential men – here representing the Executive Committee for the important Church Bazaar of 1910.

Front Row L–R: Joe Preston, Headmaster of the Church School, A. J. (later Sir Alfred) Law, Dr. G. Kinkaid Pitcairn, Rev. Dr. Salts, Vicar of Littleborough, Rev. C. E. Davis, his Curate and W. H. Dixon of Benthouse (A. J. Law's Brother-in-Law).

Back Row L–R: W. Kay, J. Stott, W. B. Pilling, E. B. Clegg of Shore, W. Bamford (A. J. Law's Secretary) and F. Kershaw.

(Below) The Ladies of the Doll Stall (L–R): Miss P. Molesworth, Mrs. G. K. Pitcairn, Miss G. Blakelock.

Left and opposite:

From the Bazaar Handbook: In addition to the musical offerings shown above there were also dramatic performances, children's entertainment, competitions and "Rev. C. E. Davis' Concerts by Masked Performers".

Entertainments.

Selections will be given daily in the Bazaar Room by

MR. F. JACKSON'S STRING BAND.

. . from 3-30 till 5, and from 6 till 10. . .

All other Entertainments will be given in the Large Room on the Ground Floor. Admission 2d. & 3d.

ENTERTAINMENT COMMITTEE. . . . Messrs. W. Bamford, C. Fletcher, W. Howarth, A. Clegg, W. Simpson, E. Rogers, H. Horrocks, W. Kershaw, G. Howarth, W. Kay, J. Stott, C. H. Howarth, J. Crossley, R. Howarth, G. R. Forshaw, J. Fairburn, H. Green, E. Leach, F. Haigh, F. Kershaw, W. B. Pilling.

FAIRY POST OFFICE, MANAGED BY GIRLS' FRIENDLY SOCIETY. LETTERS DESPATCHED AT ANY HOUR. CHARGE 1d.

Opening Ceremony—Thursday, Feb. 3rd. 1910.

REV. A. SALTS, LL.D.,
VICAR AND BAZAAR PRESIDENT.

The Bazaar will be opened at 3 p.m. by . . .

Mrs. C. R. N. Beswicke-Royds

OF PYKE HOUSE.

And an Address given by

Mrs. Knox,

OF BISHOP'S COURT, MANCHESTER.

Chairman - Rev. Dr. Salts.

SLADEN MILL

Sladen Mill stood on one of the earliest recorded water-powered sites in Littleborough. The photographs (Left) show the remarkably modern-looking structure at the height of its (and the textile industry's) prosperity. The millowner's house stands on the hillside above the mill and the whitewashed building is the Woodcock Inn – also known (appropriately, since it crouched in Lydgate Clough) as "Th 'Gap". The Gap formed by the clough was bridged by an embankment during the construction of the 'new' Halifax Turnpike and it is from there that this photograph was taken.

The scene is vastly different now. The mill (Below) was destroyed by fire, the house and inn demolished and the bare piece of ground between the curving road and the confluence of Lydgate and Castle Clough Brooks is shaded by mature trees. The business – of dyeing and finishing – survived the fire and the mill was rebuilt (though not in so fine a style). 'Kershaw's' gave way to 'Courtauld's' and the mill was finally closed down in 1980.

Lydgate Mill, another early site using the water of Lydgate Brook to power its machinery stood at the other (western) end of the Clough; eventually owned by Law's of Durn it closed in about 1970. Here too there was a pub conveniently situated alongside the mill – and also on the Old Blackstonedge Turnpike. This pub, the Gate Inn (Right) held the oldest recorded License for any Inn in the Rochdale Division. It closed in 1943 but was re-opened as the Lydgate Inn in 1975.

So, after two hundred years of industrial development and decline Lydgate Clough is reverting to what it once was – a quiet, steep sided, tree-shrouded valley, pushing up from the valley floor to the heights of Blackstonedge.

The railway in Lancashire and Yorkshire Days. Note the low-level platform in the photograph (Left). This was a standard feature of early stations and Littleborough's platform was only raised to near – but not quite – modern height very recently.

The entrance to Summit Tunnel is familiar and the 'chair and block and bull-head' rail will be familiar to railway enthusiasts. But what are the curious instruments being prominently displayed by these Lancashire and Yorkshire Railway workmen?

The men of the Volunteer Fire Brigade pose for an official photograph outside the newly-acquired Council Offices. The horses were those used by the Council for its general work and had to be collected from various locations before they could be hitched to the fire engine.

The gleaming new appliance is lettered "Littleborough Local Board Fire Brigade" – the 'Board' title being used before the more familiar 'Urban District' was adopted.

FALCON HOTEL

(Opposite Page) A procession makes its way through the decorated Square. The community came together readily to celebrate national events, locally-sponsored celebrations like the annual Cycle Parade and, of course, the Whit Walks (held on the Friday of Whit Week, not the more familiar Monday).

A Carnival, held in conjunction with "Shopping Week" and organised by the local Traders' Association was a popular feature in the 1930s and the Carnival was revived in the 1960s outside the framework of Shopping Week. A recent institution is a "Village Fete" organised annually by local community groups.

Apart from the tram wires and support standards (and the blackened buildings) the street-scene is much the same today, but the processions passing through The Square may be very different. (Right) A portion of the Trans-Pennine Anti Nuclear March of Easter 1981.

(Below): A trip on a canal barge was a popular holiday event in the years before 1920. Here the Rechabites leave Littleborough Wharf in 1915. Probably they were heading along the 'Long Pound', the three mile lock-free level to Rochdale and on to Hartley Farm, Ashfield Valley, then a rural spot, where refreshments could be obtained.

The Cycle Parade was a popular annual event in Littleborough before 1914. The 1911 parade (Left) comes down Hare Hill Road, the leading cart advertising Dances at the Conservative Club and Co-op Hall (in Bare Hill Street). The Tradesman's entry (Opposite) representing 'Coal' and complete with small boy carrying miner's lamp and brew-can won a prize – albeit a Second! (Top Right). The parade crosses the bridge after coming down Halifax Road. Looking at this area today it is almost impossible to believe that there were two shops (the canopied building on the left) sited between the river and the entrance to Ebor Street. And looking at the police officer escorting the parade on the left one must surely acknowledge the debt Modern Man owes to the electric iron and crease-resistant fabrics!

A different but equally important occasion was the Co-operative Society Children's Gala (Below Left). Here, a procession swings out of Hare Hill Road round the corner of the Co-op building and into Sale Street. By the time this photograph was taken the Co-op Hall had been added to the older 'Store' building.

Before the days of the internal combustion engine – the age of literal Horse-power-horses like these were an indispensible part of life; raw cotton and wool to the mills, finished goods from the mills to the railway, wagon after wagon of coal from the railway sidings to the Gasworks in Hare Hill Road, hooves and iron-shod wagon wheels making a deafening noise on the granite setts of the streets.

Occasionally, as here (Bottom Right) they were carefully groomed and decorated, their harness polished until it gleamed and the workday horses were On Show, possibly for a parade. Here they are seen lined up on the parcel of land between the river and the railway station. The absence of trees is noticeable; just a few – presumably newly-planted – on the station approach.

HOLLINGWORTH - LAKE - ROCHDALE.
STAGE.
LANDING STAGE, LAKE H
LAKE HOTEL.
DANCE FLOOR
CLARA CLARA

The Rochdale Canal was first proposed in 1766 and one of the early promoters was Colonel Beswicke-Royds of Pike House, Littleborough, but argument and controversy delayed the final Parliamentary sanction until 1794. The intervening years brought a number of alternative proposals, one of which envisaged taking the canal up Lydgate Clough and through a long tunnel under Blackstonedge to emerge in the Ryburn valley at Rishworth.

The final Canal Act made one important proviso; instead of the 'Narrow' canal originally proposed, the canal was to be built to 'Broad' standards, capable of taking barges 70′ long by 14′ beam, rather than the 7′ beam narrow boats. Work began at Sowerby Bridge in 1794 and by the end of 1798 the canal was completed from there to Rochdale and by 1804 it had reached Manchester.

Not only was the Rochdale Canal the first canal across the Pennines it was by far the most successful of the three canals linking Lancashire and Yorkshire and in its peak years in the 1880s carried about three-quarters of a million tonnes annually. The pictures here show typical scenes in the canal age. Mills and factories alongside the canal had their own wharves; the one illustrated (Top) served the coal and clay workings under Cleggswood Hill alongside Hollingworth Road. Ben Healey Bridge stood at the end of the Wharf used by barges unloading at Littleborough and was at one time reached by a level crossing over the railway. The barge in the photograph (Right) of Summit West Lock is on the Summit level of the canal, 600′ above sea-level. Many sections of the canal are still navigable although the whole is closed to navigation; the Summit level is used for a trail-boat rally every year and Long Lees Lock at the other end of this section has been restored by volunteers. Much restoration has been carried out in the Rochdale area and some at Sowerby Bridge and the eventual aim is to restore the trans-Pennine link to full navigational standards and add it to the network of 2000 miles of Inland Waterways in the country.

The Rochdale Canal needed vast reservoirs to supply it with water. Most were high on the moors above Littleborough but one, Hollingworth, was more accessible and became a popular rendezvous as early as the 1860s.

With the coming of the Cheap Day Rail Excursion and the family car it declined in popularity, but is now the centre of a Country Park; of the 193 such parks in the country, Hollingworth is in the Top Ten, with something like 250,000 visitors annually. The photograph on the opposite page shows it in the less crowded days of the inter-war years.

Roads, Canal and Railway were responsible for the development of Littleborough, and Ealees Road (Left) may have been the line of the early Blackstonedge Road – before the building of the canal forced a diversion. School House, on the left was the site for Littleborough's first School, Helliwell's Endowed and Cromwell Cottage (Right) has several curious but unconfirmed Civil War legends attached to it.

The Rake Inn (Below Left) stands at the junction of the Old and New Blackstonedge roads and an earlier packhorse track climbed the hill by way of Windybank on the hill above.

"Gale" Road (Below Right) – more correctly Todmorden Road was not built until 1824 when the construction of the canal had successfully drained the marshy valley-bottom; this was just one year before the opening of the Stockton and Darlington railway which heralded a new age in transport. The photograph shown here was taken before 1905 (when the electric tramway was extended to Summit). Note also the old Vicarage for Holy Trinity Church which stood on a cramped site between the road and the chancel which had been built in 1888.

Photographs of Rochdale's trams are not all that common, and photographs of the trams in operation are very rare indeed.

Here we see two standard four-wheeled tramcars (the most usual type) passing on the loop at the junction of Featherstall Road and Whitelees Road. Much of the tramway was single-track with passing loops and one car had to wait (here it is the Littleborough-bound one) until the one coming in the opposite direction arrived – hopefully on time.

Steam trams began running in Littleborough in 1882, operated by the ponderously-named "Manchester, Bury, Rochdale and Oldham Tramways Company". The company's lines (which in fact never reached Manchester) were in two parts and laid to two gauges – the standard 4′ 8½″ (similar to railway track) in Oldham and from there to Royton; from Royton to Rochdale and in the Rochdale area they were the narrow 3′ 6″ gauge.

The long covered-top bogie cars were hauled by a squat steam locomotive; at the terminus (in the case of Littleborough alongside the Parish Church), the locomotive ran round a loop ready to haul the car back to Rochdale.

The private operators were "municipalised" in the early 1900s with a view to introducing electric trams. The narrow gauge tracks were taken up and standard-gauge laid down and the first electric trams ran from Rochdale to Littleborough in May 1905. They first terminated at the junction of Church Street and Hare Hill Road – until the complicated triangle of tracks was laid out in The Square in connection with the extension to Summit in August 1905.

Summit was the terminus not only of the Rochdale tramways, but of the whole of the vast South Lancashire Tramway network. From here it was possible in theory to run a standard-gauge tram all the way to Liverpool, to Altrincham or to Hazel Grove on the South side of Stockport. The arrival of the trams at Summit posed a problem for the neighbouring authority of Todmorden. They had standard gauge trams on one side and the narrow Halifax gauge on the other. If they chose to introduce trams, which gauge should they choose?

Todmorden solved the problem by introducing motor buses (and were only the second town in Britain to do so, Eastbourne being the first). The buses arrived in December 1906 but judiciously, Todmorden chose not to register them until the first day of the new tax year and the services started on January 1st 1907. Todmorden's buses still terminated at Summit long after Rochdale scrapped the trams and it was not until the coming of West Yorkshire PTE and GMT that buses from Todmorden began running down from Summit to Littleborough on a regular basis.

Opposite Page: (Top Left) A Steam tram ready to leave The Square for Rochdale.
(Bottom Left) The first electric tram to run into Littleborough, May 24th 1905 seen here near the first terminus in Church Street.

This Page: (Left) The first tram to Summit, August 1905.
(Below Left) Laying the complicated triangle of trackwork in connection with the electrification and extension to Summit, August 1905.
(Below) The abandonment notice when Rochdale Corporation replaced the trams by buses.

ROCHDALE CORPORATION PASSENGER TRANSPORT DEPARTMENT.

NOTICE.

ABANDONMENT OF TRAMWAYS & SUBSTITUTION OF MOTOR OMNIBUS SERVICES.

ROCHDALE, SMALLBRIDGE, LITTLEBOROUGH AND SUMMIT SECTIONS.

From Sunday, 19th October, 1930, the service of Tram Cars on the above routes will be withdrawn and substituted by a service of Motor Omnibuses.

For Fares, Stages and Time-Tables see other bills.

Tramways Offices,
Mellor Street, Rochdale.
8th October, 1930.

GEO. WEBSTER,
General Manager.

(Left) An almost dream-like photograph of Hollingworth Lake at this time. The Pump House which drew the water from the lake up to the level of the feeder channel leading to Summit is prominent in the picture.

The Last Edwardian Year – and the End of an Era. Littleborough's Cricket Team which won the Central Lancashire League Championship that year and the Parish Church Procession of 1910. (Below)

The Littleborough of the 1930s.

The Littleborough Band assembled outside Calder Cottage (Below) and a lorry owned by Clegg's Mill at Rakewood (Right).

The Depression Years were unpleasant ones for Littleborough, though not as disastrous a period as elsewhere. Some mills closed – notably Frankfort and West View at Durn, never to re-open but its claim to be a small town of many industries helped to cushion the worst effects of the trade recession.

SORSBY & Cº COAL MERCHANTS.
LITTLEBOROUGH

The panorama (Left) shows Littleborough in about 1930, before the development of housing on the high ground at Shore and Calderbrook.

Much of the recent development has been to the South of the town, around Smithy Bridge and Dearnley; the population of Littleborough, static for years at about 12,000 fell by 1961 to about 10,000. New development brought about a rapid increase in size and now the town is, at something approaching 14,000 people bigger than ever before. This contrasts sharply with other towns in the area. Todmorden, for instance, which once had about 20,000 inhabitants is now little bigger than Littleborough.

The aerial view (Above) taken in 1926 shows lines of wagons in the railway sidings and the half-finished Spenwood Tannery buildings. Python Mill stands adjacent to its mill lodge and a tram is seen making its way along Church Street. The Gasworks is prominent *top left* and beyond it the old Hare Hill Mill, cutting into the line of Hare Hill Road.

Sandbagged Council Offices (Left), soldiers billeted at West View Mill and Sun Mill, Featherstall, evacuees from Manchester billeted on local families, an anti-aircraft battery at Hollingworth Lake and redundant canal narrow boats moored to form booms across the reservoirs on Blackstonedge (to prevent, they said, seaplanes from landing!), "Wings For Victory" and "Salute The Soldier" savings weeks, "Holidays at Home", "Shelter Drill" for children, "Dig For Victory", bombers jettisoning unwanted bombs on the moors (though not, mercifully, on the town itself), sympathy for the refugee Lehmanns, Oppenheims, Picards and Treuherzes plus a little harmless black-marketeering (and "off-ration" bacon, it was rumoured, stored in the cells at the Police Station). This was Littleborough's War.

The Auxiliary Fire Service supplemented the regular brigade during the War years in the same way the War Reserve supplemented the Police. Small pumps like these were towed behind any variety of vehicle. Note the white-lining around the mudguards and along the running board of the car. Note also the elaborate visor on the headlamp. This allowed a tiny pool of light to fall directly in front of the vehicle; fortunately the speed-limit in the Blackout was a mere 15 mph.

(Opposite) Men's coach trip about to leave the Roundhouse for a day out, June 1930.

CAFE
MITCHELL
HIPPODROME
BALLARD BROWN

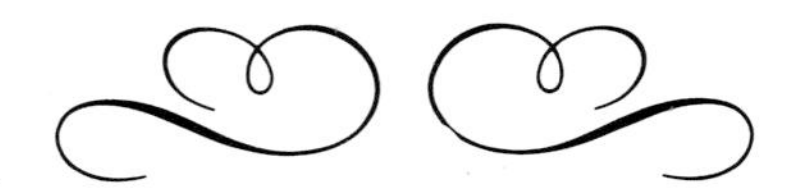

Acknowledgements

Our thanks go to Austin W. Colligan for his research and notes connected with the photographs and events described. We also wish to acknowledge the generous assistance given by Alan Luke and the members and friends of the Littleborough Historical Society.

Many local people have contributed to the book – directly, by providing information and photographs, indirectly by way of comments, memories and half-forgotten anecdotes. Our sincere thanks to all of them.

Our thanks must go also to the unknown Victorian and Edwardian photographers who have provided us with such splendid material – and far more than it is possible to include in one volume.

The heavy photographic plate and cumbersome camera gave way to the Kodak Brownie and roll-film, photography became a popular hobby and the tradition of local interest photography died.

Every family now has its own record of local events and in that collection there may be photographs every bit as important to future generations as these Edwardian photographs are to ours. Perhaps you have photographs of local interest taken during the past fifty years – Whit Walks, the Carnivals of the 1930s sponsored by the Traders' Association, records of severe winters, Wartime activities, – even air-raid shelters and static water tanks – post-war 'Utility' buses, typical family groups (and how about the Men of the National Service Generation?), the construction of the Trans-Pennine Motorway and so on.

If you have such photographs the Publisher of this book would like to hear from you.